HAVANA

HAVANA

ARLINDA MIRANDA

SMITHMARK

This edition published in 1995 by SMITHMARK Publishers Inc., a division of U.S. Media Holdings, Inc. 16 East 32nd Street, New York, New York 10016

SMITHMARK books are available for bulk purchase for sales promotion and premium use. For details write or telephone the Manager of Special Sales, SMITHMARK Publishers Inc., 16 East 32nd Street, New York, NY 10016. (212) 532-6600.

Produced by Brompton Books Corp., 15 Sherwood Place, Greenwich, CT 06830.

ISBN 0-8317-2152-9

Printed in China

10 9 8 7 6 5 4 3 2 1

1 Palm trees and grand architecture create a beautiful square in Old Havana.

2-3 The *El Galleon* cruises past the sixteenth-century Castillo del Morro.

4 The Gulf of Mexico's brilliant blue water laps against the shore of Havana.

5 The ruins of once impressive buildings hint at the grandeur of Havana's past.

Acknowledgments
The publisher would like to thank Amy Buskirk, the editor, Sue Rose, the designer, and Simon Shelmerdine for production. The following individuals and agencies provided photographic material:

© **Robert Baldridge, pages:** 4, 5, 12-13, 14, 15, 18, 19, 20, 21, 29, 32, 34, 36-7, 39, 40, 42, 43, 44, 45, 46-7, 50, 51, 52, 53, 54-5, 58-9, 60, 61, 62, 63, 65, 71, 74, 75, 76, 77, 78-9, 80, 81, 82, 83, 84-5, 86, 87, 90, 91, 92, 93, 94-5, 96
Life File/Juliet Highet, pages: 2-3, 11, 17, 30-1, 35, 41
Life File/Jeremy Hoare, pages: 1, 16, 18, 22-3, 24, 25, 26-7, 28, 33, 48, 49, 57, 64, 66, 67, 68-9, 72-3, 88, 89

CONTENTS

INTRODUCTION

From its grand colonial past to its international glamour days as a sophisticated resort, to its present as the domain of Fidel Castro and one of the last communist states, Havana has maintained its allure throughout its rich history. A fun-loving resilient people and an unsurpassed tropical beauty make Cuba, and especially its intriguing capital, an irresistible destination.

The largest island of the Greater Antilles, Cuba was discovered by Christopher Columbus, whose scribe recorded in 1492, "the island is very large and so lovely, that he was never weary of speaking well of it." Spain became the dominant influence in Cuba and there is little trace of the Indians who predated them. Peaceful among themselves, the Indian tribes of Cuba resisted the Spanish incursion, but were no match for the advancing conquistadores. Diego Velázquez, commissioned by Spain to find gold, became the island's first governor and established several garrison towns including Villa de San Cristobal de la Habana, believed to have been founded in 1515. Later known simply as La Habana in Spanish, Havana, with its excellent deep harbor, became the Cuban capital and the navigation center for imperial Spain in the Americas.

Gold was mined in Cuba, and tobacco was grown, but over the years sugar became and has remained the mainstay of the Cuban economy. Havana flourished as a port with ships loading up on sugar and tobacco bound for Europe. As the demand for these crops grew, so did Havana. As the city prospered, the threat of attack from pirates and other European ships was ever present. To protect their busy port, the Spaniards built the great fortresses of Castillo del Morro and Castillo de la Punta on either side of the channel leading into the harbor. An enormous chain was stretched between the two and raised at night to prevent plunderers from reaching Havana. By the late 1500s, Havana was one of the most populous cities in the new world. Increasingly lavish private dwellings designed around courtyards with balconies and fountains, as well as churches and public plazas of great beauty were built. Havana was growing in range and depth well beyond her beginnings as an outpost for trade.

As trade grew, the Spanish brought slaves from West Africa to work the gold mines and the sugar and tobacco plantations of Cuba. By the mid 1520s, large numbers of

African slaves began arriving in Cuba to supply the needed labor. The slave trade grew with the demand for cane sugar. The Spanish crown maintained a tight control on the Cuban economy by means of taxes, tariffs, trade, and even production restrictions throughout this time. Despite several armed revolts, the Spaniards prevailed and no change in trade policies for their Cuban colony occurred. Resentment, however, grew.

In 1762 the British captured Havana and held it for almost a year. During that time the British, intending to make Havana a free port, relaxed trade restrictions between Cuba and their North American Colonies, resulting in an even greater demand for sugar. An exchange for the Spanish-occupied Florida peninsula was arranged with the British, and Cuba returned to the Spanish Empire. Although Spain continued to dominate Cuban trade, the year of British occupation had strengthened Cuba's relationship with the British Colonies of North America, a tie that was to grow.

When the Colonies declared their independence from England in 1776, Spain supported them and allowed North American trade with Cuba. The demand for sugar grew, and by the end of the eighteenth century Cuba became the center for the Caribbean sugar trade. More slaves were imported to meet the demand in the fields, and by 1830 the West African slaves outnumbered the whites. Spain brutally repressed any slave rebellions, but the cost was great and slavery was finally abolished in Cuba in 1880. It is interesting to note that slaves in Cuba, despite their undeniably harsh conditions, had some advantages over slaves in other countries such as the right to marry, own and sell crops or crafts and, for a lucky few, to use their money to buy their freedom. All children born of slave and colonist were free at birth, and it was often free blacks who helped the slaves revolt.

At a time when most of South America was being liberated by Simón Bolívar, Cuba remained part of the Spanish Empire. There were those, mainly in Havana, who wanted to maintain the link to Spain and others, including many sugar planters, who wanted greater ties to the United States. There was even talk of Cuba becoming an American state. It was José Martí, an exiled journalist, poet and philosopher who, believing in equality for all Cubans, led the way to the country's brief term of independence. With the cooperation of General Máximo Gomez, Martí led the revolt against Spain in 1895. The fighting between Cuba and Spain left tens of thousands dead on each side, including Martí himself. The United States, concerned for its own citizens and their extensive investments there, sent its battleship, *Maine*, to the Bay of Havana. In 1898 the ship was mysteriously sunk with its crew aboard, and the United States declared war on Spain.

The Spanish-American War lasted about a year and was fought mainly in Cuba. The stories of malaria, yellow fever and Teddy Roosevelt and his Rough Riders charging up San Juan Hill are legendary. The Spanish officially left Cuba on New Year's Day 1899. The Americans also left, but not before stripping General Gomez of his title and disarming his troops. Further, the Americans presented the new republic with its constitution, which was modeled on the United States Constitution and written in Washington. The new Cuban Constitution included the Platt Amendment, which gave the United States the right to intervene in Cuba whenever it felt the island's independence, and its own interests there, were threatened. At this time the United States also arranged the 99-year lease of Guantánamo Bay Naval Base, which it still holds. Finally, with a framework of pro-American democracy in place, the United States withdrew from Cuba. Its overwhelming influence, however, continued.

After a series of largely ineffectual and corrupt administrations, Cuba's nominal independence, precarious in part due to the economic swings caused by a one-crop economy, came to an end. Colonel Fulgencio Batista, with the backing of United States Ambassador Sumner Welles, took control in 1933. From World War I through the 1950s Havana's reputation as the Latin-American center of luxurious casinos, extravagant night clubs and seaside hotels flourished. So did government corruption.

Tourists, and especially Americans, spent lavishly in Havana. The country prospered and many Cubans attained a level of middle class comfort unknown in other parts of Latin America. There were, however, many social problems, and much of the countryside failed to benefit from the prosperity enjoyed in Havana. Batista, by now a self-proclaimed general, managed to suppress unrest until Fidel Castro, along with the legendary Che Guevara, through a series of guerrilla attacks finally managed to drive the dictator into exile on New Year's Day 1959.

Castro quickly took control of the economy, nationalized large plantations and seized American-owned assets. The United States retaliated with an economic boycott and severed diplomatic relations. Castro, however, found economic and ideological support from the Soviet Union, which remained his financial backer for thirty years until its own troubles prevented further assistance. The United States made many attempts over the years to topple the regime, from the disastrous CIA-sponsored Bay of Pigs invasion to numerous assassination attempts on Castro. Tensions reached a high point in 1962 with the Cuban Missile Crisis when President Kennedy, responding to the finding of Russian missiles deployed in Cuba and aimed at the United States, ordered an American naval blockade of the island which ultimately resulted in the removal of these missiles from Cuba in return for the removal of American missiles from Turkey. Until Khrushchev and Kennedy reached agreement, the Cuban Missile Crisis threatened the possibility of nuclear war. The confrontation passed, but Cuba has remained a sore subject in Washington.

Despite the American embargo, and the exodus of hundreds of thousands of Cuban citizens, especially the educated professionals, Castro has had amazing staying power. While Cuba remains a closed society, and allows no dissent, socialism in the sunshine has a different flavor than its counterparts elsewhere. Despite rationing, and the constant need to queue for virtually everything, the Cuban people remain outgoing and fun-loving. In an effort to foster economic growth, the government today actively encourages tourism and many travelers are re-discovering the lure of Havana. Hotels have been built and some of the old ones refurbished. The climate, the people, the mystique of Havana beckons.

ARCHITECTURE

Visitors to Cuba today are struck by the contrasts between the very old, the modern, and the many decaying buildings of Havana. The need for repair and even paint is apparent everywhere. Havana suffers not only a financial crisis, but also the difficulty of assimilating her opulent architectural past into the more utilitarian needs of its present-day socialist society. Sadly, in the case of many formerly luxurious private residences, architectural treasures are left to crumble.

The grace and beauty of sixteenth- and seventeenth-century colonial Spanish architecture in the oldest part of the city, known as La Havana Vieja, or Old Havana, is so unparalleled as to have been declared a World Heritage Site by UNESCO. With the help of Spain and international funds through UNESCO, this part of Havana has had some help with restoration.

Known for its many gracious plazas, Havana is adorned with fountains and statues of its heroes. The Capitolio, a replica of the United States Capitol Building, is an evocative reminder of the scope of American influence in Havana's past, just as the bleakness of the Soviet-designed structures tell of that country's imprint on the city. The mix of cultures apparent in Havana's architectural variety gives evidence of her dramatic history and adds to the city's fascination.

11 Many of Havana's buildings may be in disrepair, but their elegance lingers.

12-13 The imposing baroque Cathedral of Havana is a fine example of the influence of Spanish Catholicism upon the city's architecture and culture.

14 Prompted by continued pirate raids, the
Spanish constructed Castillo de la Punta at
the mouth of Havana's harbor in the late
sixteenth century.

15 The Spanish hoped the Castillo del Morro
along with its complement, the Castillo de la
Punta, would deter attacks on the city.

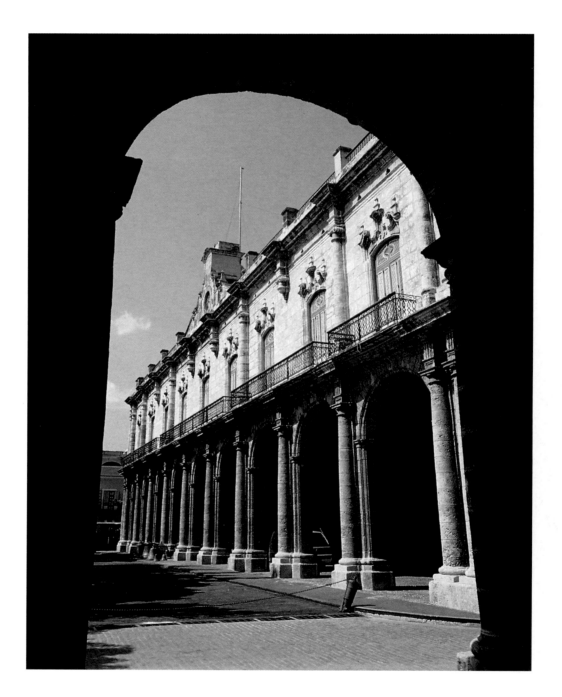

16 The majestic Captain General's Palace, completed in 1791, served as the home of the Spanish colonial governors.

17 The Castillo de la Real Fuerza speaks of the continued Spanish concern about invaders, but its thick walls and moat were useless in defending the city from French pirates.

18 The Palaces of Conde Combillo and the
Marquéses de Arcos, built in the eighteenth
century, are persisting symbols of the fantastic
wealth of the Spanish.

19 The Colón Cemetery is crowded with ornate architecture and sculpture honoring the dead.

20 The National Theater combines art
nouveau and neoclassical styles to create a
stunning structure. It is home to Cuba's
national ballet and opera companies.

21 A closer look at the National Theater's facade reveals the beautifully carved stone that adorns the building.

22-23 Havana's grand old buildings take on a golden glow at dusk.

21

24 The Hotel Plaza was converted from a
private residence into a hotel in 1909 to take
advantage of the booming tourist industry.

25 The interior of the National Hotel hints at the luxuriance sought by wealthy holidaymakers in the first half of the twentieth century. Today, it is still an elegant residence for tourists.

26-27 The former Presidential Palace, home to a series of corrupt presidents, has served as the Museum of the Revolution since the victory of the Fidelistas.

28 Ernest Hemingway spent many years of his life in Havana, and tourists are encouraged to dine in his favorite restaurant or become inebriated in his preferred bar. His luxurious home is kept as a museum devoted to his life and work.

29 Havana is blessed with dozens of plazas. The brilliant white marble of the Fountain of Lions graces the San Francisco Square.

30-31 In the mid 1950s, the land along Havana's west shore saw an influx of money. Wealthy investors, including American gangsters, backed numerous casinos and hotels. The Revolution banned gambling and curtailed tourism, but these reminders of a decadent past remain.

32 Although many of the civic buildings retain
their former grandeur, the majority of Havana's
residences tell a different story. Most are
overcrowded and in disrepair.

33 Humans abandoned this building long
ago; it is now home to tenacious plants.

34 A huge marble obelisk, dedicated to the hero José Martí, dominates Revolution Square. Castro often uses a stand below the monument to speak to the Cuban people.

35 Political symbols and slogans decorate many of Havana's buildings.

36-37 The Capitolio was completed under the corrupt president Gerardo Machado in 1929. Its marble halls have been rejected by the current government and now house the Academy of Sciences.

STREET SCENES

Encouraged by a warm climate and refreshing tropical breezes, Cubans have always liked *la calle*, or to be out and about as we would less succinctly put it in English. The streets of Havana are always lively. Music is an integral part of Cuban life and the African beat coupled with the Spanish guitar make for a distinctively rich musical heritage. Music, of course, provides the opportunity for that favorite Cuban enterprise, dance. Be it rumba, merengue or whatever, even the austerities of socialism cannot keep the Cubans from dancing. Festivals give further opportunities to dress up and dance.

Shopping, especially because of the endless queues, gives another dimension to street life in Havana. Naturally gregarious, Cubans are adaptive in often changing even a tedious wait into a social occasion. As Cuba is not a consumer society, visitors looking for the usual variety of goods found in Caribbean resort areas will be disappointed. Colorful crafts, however, displayed in open air markets are available for purchase. For most Westerners, looking through what passes for stores in Havana is, if nothing else, an educational experience.

The streets of Havana are also famous for the large variety of old American cars, lovingly preserved. Because of the economic boycott and the notorious difficulty obtaining spare parts, these cars are treasured.

39 On a sunny day, La Rampa, one of the most famous streets in Havana, is crowded with shoppers and people relaxing in the warm sun.

40 On New Year's Eve, Havana's people celebrate the Triumph of the Revolution by decorating the streets with the national flag and chains made from tin cans.

41 Children, clad in colorful costumes, dance to celebrate the anniversary of Castro's army entering Cuba.

42 Although the Revolutionary government has made religious worship difficult, and religious holidays are not celebrated officially, Havana becomes a site of joyous celebration on Christmas Day. A man on stilts entertains the carnival crowds.

43 Two girls show off their brightly colored clothing.

44 Boys dance and laugh in celebration of Christmas.

45 The African influence on Cuban culture can clearly be seen in this carnival costume.

46-47 Combining African and Spanish traditions, this folklorico group provides entertainment to the crowds gathered on the streets for Christmas Day.

48 Musicians, playing traditional Cuban
music, serenade the customers of a streetside
cafe.

49 Waiting in a line for scarce consumer
products and necessities is a regrettably
frequent occurrence for Havana's people.

50 At the outdoor market on the Avenue of Presidents, shoppers can find a wide variety of goods including attractive handmade baskets and chairs.

51 Artisans often use local material to create their products. Palm fronds make beautiful, as well as functional, hats and containers.

52 During the heyday before the Revolution, Cuba imported more American cars than any other nation in the world. Since the American blockade has severely reduced the entry of new automobiles, Cubans put a remarkable effort into keeping their cars in good repair.

53 The highly polished body of a classic car gleams in the Havana sun.

54-55 The number of vintage cars on Havana's streets often astound tourists, but they are a typical sight.

NIGHTLIFE

Renowned for its sugar, cigars and rum, Havana is also famous for its nightlife. Although not as extravagantly decadent as it once was, even present-day Havana can put on quite a show at night. The island's often naturally flamboyant people, have a unique tradition of musical rhythms and love to entertain. Nightlife in Havana, if not quite what it once was, is still an energetic, joyous, and particularly Cuban celebration of life.

Tropicana, a legendary Havana nightclub, now presents productions reminiscent of the 1950s with extravagant costumes and scores of dancers. Cuban music is everywhere and even small local bars are alive with the distinctive Cuban beat. Music and dancing can be found throughout Havana on a variety of levels for tourists and locals alike.

Nightlife in Havana must include a drive or stroll along the Malecón, Havana's beautiful drive and promenade, which runs for miles along the ocean and is a favorite romantic spot. Life may be harsh in socialist Cuba, but surely the beauties and rhythms of Havana at night belie life's daytime austerities. Spanish, American and Russian influences can be seen in many facets of Havana, but its nightlife is truly a reflection of its own originality.

57 As the sun sets, Havana's people are relieved of the day's blazing heat, and the city assumes a magical glow.

58-59 At night, the neon signs of restaurants and the lights of passing cars colorfully illuminate Monserrate Street.

60 Drums, guitars and violins may be the
traditional instruments of Cuba, but these
resourceful buskers have chosen to earn their
money playing bagpipes.

61 On New Year's Eve, young people make
merry on the Malecón, Havana's seaside
drive.

66 The Tropicana Nightclub may provide
flashy entertainment, but for local people who
can't afford the Tropicana's exorbitant prices,
the Salón Rosado provides a place to dance
and listen to live music.

67 Most nights the Salón Rosado's dance
floor is packed with enthusiastic dancers.

68-69 The lights of La Rampa lead to the
quiet night sea.

PEOPLE

The people of Havana are multi-racial, descended from the Spaniards who colonized the island, as well as from the West African slaves brought in to work the fields. An Asian influence is also seen, coming from the indentured Chinese workers, who were brought to Cuba during the late 1800s when support for slavery was collapsing. While there remain many "pure" blacks, Chinese and Europeans, much mingling of races is evident in the faces of Havana. Cubans are said to possess a northern work ethic in addition to their tropical sense of fun. It is a unique combination and one which has served them well in the face of hardship. The resilient people of Havana have experienced a range from great excess to lean times and shortages. Originally dominated by Spain, they came to be influenced by the economic powers of first the United States and then the Soviet Union, all the while maintaining a strong sense of themselves.

Cubans are warm and tend to be effusive. Spanish is their language and they speak very quickly, often dropping the end letters and running words together. The people are demonstrative and will often use their hands to make a point, frequently reaching out and touching the person to whom they are speaking. Flamboyant, naturally charming and generous, everyone remembers the people of Havana.

A natural draw for travelers, this lively city and its people never cease to attract, fascinate, and charm. As the Cuban government turns to promoting tourism as a means of improving the country's economic situation, it is the people of Havana who assure us that just as this exotic city was once considered the most popular destination in the Caribbean, surely it will be so again.

71 Two youths take a break in the sun near Havana's harbor.

72-73 Children wearing brightly colored uniforms march to one of Cuba's state supported schools.

74 Baseball, as popular in Cuba as it is in the
United States, forms a major pastime for
children.

75 Cubans watch baseball religiously, and the
players are much respected.

76 The melding of different peoples into one country is shown on a small scale in this group of children.

77 Like children the world over, Havana's are eager to have their picture taken.

78-79 The Malecón with its beautiful views and warm ocean breezes is a romantic locale.

80 A vendor tests his product in the outdoor market in Havana's Chinatown.

81 Stall keepers in Havana's markets offer a variety of fresh fruits and vegetables.

82 Since the sixteenth century, tobacco has been one of Cuba's most important exports, and Cuban cigars are coveted throughout the world. In the Fábrica de Tabacos Partagás, they are still made by hand.

83 Workers roll the tobacco leaves to form the prized cigars.

84-5 Talented musicians and dancers form one of Havana's top folklorico groups.

86 The Hotel Copacabana combines athletics and entertainment in its ballet aquatics team.

87 The sea still plays an important role in the lives of Havana's people. On a dinner boat, a sailor has the opportunity to ply his ancient craft.

88 A soldier walks along a sun-drenched street. From its infancy as a ragged army of rebels, the military has played an important role in Revolutionary Cuba.

89 In 1955, while Castro was in exile in Mexico, he met Che Guevara who went on to become one of Cuba's heroes. An iconic portrait of this popular figure hangs above a doorway from which old men watch the world go by.

90 Given the shortage of fuel and spare parts for motorized vehicles, pedicabs have become a common way to avoid a walk on Havana's hot streets.

91 A cement step along La Rampa provides a welcome spot for a rest.

92 A couple enjoys a makeshift picnic on the Avenue of Presidents.

93 Weddings in Havana create an excuse for extravagant clothes and celebration.

94-95 On a warm, sunny day there can be no better location for a bicycle ride than the Malecón.

96 Havana's next generation is poised to continue the city's traditions and to mold its future.